Dad & Daughter Journal

By: Iona Yeung

Why journal?

Dedicated to dads & their daughters out there...because there are questions your daughter wants you to ask and there are questions your dad wants you to ask him.

It's easy to get caught up with work, homework, friends...etc that you forget to take time out for family. No matter how well you think you know each other, I bet there's always more to learn.

These journal prompts are designed to strengthen the bond between a dad and daughter, to uncover things you may not know about each other before.

Because sometimes it's easier to put thoughts onto paper.

Take the time to reflect, ask questions, doodle, scribble.

To my daughter,
These are things I love about you...

i.e. sense of humour, the way you always take the time
to say goodbye before you leave...

_____

_____

_____

_____

_____

_____

_____

_____

_____

_____

_____

_____

To my dad,
These are things I love about you...

i.e. The stories you tell me about you and mom, the sandwiches you make for me...

_____

_____

_____

_____

_____

_____

_____

_____

_____

_____

_____

_____

_____

_____

To my daughter,
What is your idea of the perfect day?

i.e. I'd wake up and have pancakes for breakfast, followed by a walk with our dog, I'd then go to the park...

_____

_____

_____

_____

_____

_____

_____

_____

_____

_____

_____

To my dad,
What is your idea of the perfect day?

i.e. I'd take the day off work, sleep in til 8am, make
breakfast and head to the beach for a surf...

_____

_____

_____

_____

_____

_____

_____

_____

_____

_____

_____

_____

_____

To my daughter,
When was the last time you felt really loved?

_____

_____

_____

_____

_____

_____

_____

_____

_____

_____

_____

_____

_____

To my dad,
When was the last time you felt really loved?

_____

_____

_____

_____

_____

_____

_____

_____

_____

_____

_____

_____

To my daughter,
Do you believe in love at first sight?

_____

_____

_____

_____

_____

_____

_____

_____

_____

_____

_____

To my dad,
Do you believe in love at first sight?

_____

_____

_____

_____

_____

_____

_____

_____

_____

_____

_____

To my daughter,
What are some things you've always wanted to ask me?

_____

_____

_____

_____

_____

_____

_____

_____

_____

_____

_____

_____

To my dad,
What are some things you've always wanted to ask me?

_____

_____

_____

_____

_____

_____

_____

_____

_____

_____

_____

_____

_____

_____

To my daughter,
What's the scariest thing you've done?

_____

_____

_____

_____

_____

_____

_____

_____

_____

_____

_____

To my daughter,
What's the scariest thing you've done?

_____

_____

_____

_____

_____

_____

_____

_____

_____

_____

_____

_____

_____

To my daughter,
What's one thing you don't often tell your friends?

_____

_____

_____

_____

_____

_____

_____

_____

_____

_____

_____

To my dad,
What's one thing you don't often tell your friends?

_____

_____

_____

_____

_____

_____

_____

_____

_____

_____

_____

_____

_____

_____

To my daughter,
If you could quit school/work and do whatever you want, what would you want to do?

_____

_____

_____

_____

_____

_____

_____

_____

_____

_____

_____

To my dad,
If you could quit school/work and do whatever you want, what would you want to do?

_____

_____

_____

_____

_____

_____

_____

_____

_____

_____

_____

_____

To my daughter,
What do you admire in people your age?

_____

_____

_____

_____

_____

_____

_____

_____

_____

_____

_____

To my dad,
What do you admire in people your age?

_____

_____

_____

_____

_____

_____

_____

_____

_____

_____

_____

_____

_____

To my daughter,
What's something you'd like for us to do together?

_____

_____

_____

_____

_____

_____

_____

_____

_____

_____

_____

To my dad,
What's something you'd like for us to do together?

_____

_____

_____

_____

_____

_____

_____

_____

_____

_____

_____

_____

Questions to ask each other

In between journaling, here are some questions you can ask each other. Some ice breakers to get to know each other:

1. Do you think you and I are alike?

2. What's your best trait?

3. Do you believe in ghosts?

4. Do you think horoscopes can predict the future?

5. What's the hardest part of your day?

7. If someone could wave a magic wand, what would you wish for?

8. If you won the lottery, what would you spend it on?

9. What's the silliest thing you've ever done?

10. Do you have any regrets?

To my daughter, what does your life look like in 5 years? Doodle it.

To my dad, what does your life look like in 5 years? Doodle it.

To my daughter,
Are you good at keeping secrets?

_____

_____

_____

_____

_____

_____

_____

_____

_____

_____

_____

To my dad,
Are you good at keeping secrets?

_____

_____

_____

_____

_____

_____

_____

_____

_____

_____

_____

_____

To my daughter, do you see the glass full or empty?

Yes/No

To my dad, do you see the glass full or empty?

Yes/No

To my daughter,
If you could eat one meal for the rest of your life, which would it be?

_____

_____

_____

_____

_____

_____

_____

_____

_____

_____

_____

To my dad,
If you could eat one meal for the rest of your life, which would it be?

_____

_____

_____

_____

_____

_____

_____

_____

_____

_____

_____

_____

_____

To my daughter,
Do you believe in love at first sight?

_____

_____

_____

_____

_____

_____

_____

_____

_____

_____

_____

_____

To my dad,
Do you believe in love at first sight?

_____

_____

_____

_____

_____

_____

_____

_____

_____

_____

_____

_____

To my daughter,
If you were to learn something new, what would it be?

_____

_____

_____

_____

_____

_____

_____

_____

_____

_____

_____

To my dad,
If you were to learn something new, what would it be?

_____

_____

_____

_____

_____

_____

_____

_____

_____

_____

_____

To my daughter,
Do you have a secret talent?

_____

_____

_____

_____

_____

_____

_____

_____

_____

_____

_____

_____

To my dad,
Do you have a secret talent?

_____

_____

_____

_____

_____

_____

_____

_____

_____

_____

_____

_____

_____

To my daughter,
If the world were to end tomorrow, what would you do today?

_____

_____

_____

_____

_____

_____

_____

_____

_____

_____

_____

_____

To my dad,
If the world were to end tomorrow, what would you do today?

_____

_____

_____

_____

_____

_____

_____

_____

_____

_____

_____

_____

_____

To my daughter,
What's one daughterg you can listen to over and over again? Why?

_____

_____

_____

_____

_____

_____

_____

_____

_____

_____

_____

To my dad,
What's one daughterg you can listen to over and over again? Why?

_____

_____

_____

_____

_____

_____

_____

_____

_____

_____

_____

_____

To my daughter,
What's one movie you can watch over and over again? Why?

_____

_____

_____

_____

_____

_____

_____

_____

_____

_____

_____

To my dad,
What's one movie you can watch over and over again? Why?

_____

_____

_____

_____

_____

_____

_____

_____

_____

_____

_____

_____

_____

To my daughter,
If you could be a super hero for the day, which one would you be and why?

_____

_____

_____

_____

_____

_____

_____

_____

_____

_____

_____

_____

To my dad,
If you could be a super hero for the day,
which one would you be and why?

_____

_____

_____

_____

_____

_____

_____

_____

_____

_____

_____

_____

_____

To my daughter,
What's something that makes you sad?

_____

_____

_____

_____

_____

_____

_____

_____

_____

_____

_____

To my dad,
What's something that makes you sad?

_____

_____

_____

_____

_____

_____

_____

_____

_____

_____

_____

_____

_____

_____

To my daughter,
What's something that always makes you happy?

_____

_____

_____

_____

_____

_____

_____

_____

_____

_____

_____

_____

To my dad,
What's something that always makes you happy?

_____

_____

_____

_____

_____

_____

_____

_____

_____

_____

_____

_____

To my daughter,
What's something that always makes you sad?

_____

_____

_____

_____

_____

_____

_____

_____

_____

_____

_____

_____

To my dad,
What's something that always makes you sad?

_____

_____

_____

_____

_____

_____

_____

_____

_____

_____

_____

_____

To my daughter,
What should I do to cheer you up when you're sad?

_____

_____

_____

_____

_____

_____

_____

_____

_____

_____

_____

_____

To my dad,
What should I do to cheer you up when you're sad?

_____

_____

_____

_____

_____

_____

_____

_____

_____

_____

_____

_____

To my daughter,
What's one thing you enjoy doing together?

_____

_____

_____

_____

_____

_____

_____

_____

_____

_____

_____

_____

To my dad,
What's one thing you enjoy doing together?

_____

_____

_____

_____

_____

_____

_____

_____

_____

_____

_____

_____

_____

To my daughter,
What's on your bucket list?

_____

_____

_____

_____

_____

_____

_____

_____

_____

_____

_____

_____

To my dad,
What's on your bucket list?

_____

_____

_____

_____

_____

_____

_____

_____

_____

_____

_____

_____

_____

To my daughter,
What can I do to get to know you better?

_____

_____

_____

_____

_____

_____

_____

_____

_____

_____

_____

_____

To my dad,
What can I do to get to know you better?

_____

_____

_____

_____

_____

_____

_____

_____

_____

_____

_____

_____

To my daughter, let's play a game

Let's play again

Best 2 out of 3?

To my daughter, this is what my perfect day looks like in drawing...

To my dad, this is what my perfect day looks like in drawing...

Things for us to share

Our joint bucket list

i.e. Run our first marathon together, go on a road trip
just us two, learn a new language…

_____

_____

_____

_____

_____

_____

_____

_____

_____

_____

_____

A list of movies we can watch together

A list of books we can read and discuss

_____

_____

_____

_____

_____

_____

_____

_____

_____

_____

_____

_____

Things to do together this year

Winter

_____

_____

_____

Spring

_____

_____

_____

Summer

_____

_____

_____

Fall

_____

_____

_____

Letters

One for every month of the year

Letters to my daughter

Letters to my daughter

_____

_____

_____

_____

_____

_____

_____

_____

_____

_____

_____

_____

_____

_____

Letters to my daughter

Letters to my daughter

Letters to my daughter

Letters to my daughter

Letters to my daughter

Letters to my daughter

_____

_____

_____

_____

_____

_____

_____

_____

_____

_____

_____

_____

_____

_____

_____

_____

Letters to my daughter

Letters to my daughter

_____

_____

_____

_____

_____

_____

_____

_____

_____

_____

_____

_____

_____

_____

Letters to my daughter

Letters to my daughter

_____

_____

_____

_____

_____

_____

_____

_____

_____

_____

_____

_____

_____

_____

Letters to my dad

_____

_____

_____

_____

_____

_____

_____

_____

_____

_____

_____

_____

_____

_____

_____

_____

Letters to my dad

Letters to my dad

_____

_____

_____

_____

_____

_____

_____

_____

_____

_____

_____

_____

_____

_____

_____

_____

Letters to my dad

Letters to my dad

_____

_____

_____

_____

_____

_____

_____

_____

_____

_____

_____

_____

_____

_____

_____

Letters to my dad

_____

_____

_____

_____

_____

_____

_____

_____

_____

_____

_____

_____

_____

_____

Letters to my dad

Letters to my dad

_____

_____

_____

_____

_____

_____

_____

_____

_____

_____

_____

_____

_____

Letters to my dad

Letters to my dad

Notes & Doodles

Use this to unleash your creativity

Made in the USA
Columbia, SC
12 June 2025

59315865R00057